D1277443

What Makes Me A
MORMON?

Other titles in the What Makes Me A . . . ? series include:

What Makes Me A
MORMON?

Charles George

KIDHAVEN PRESS

An imprint of Thomson Gale, a part of The Thomson Corporation

Detroit • New York • San Francisco • San Diego • New Haven, Conn.
Waterville, Maine • London • Munich

LIBRARY OF CONGRESS CATALOGING-IN-PUBLICATION DATA

George, Charles, 1949–
    Mormon / by Charles George
        p. cm. — (What makes me a ?)
    Includes bibliographical references and index.
    Summary: Discusses Mormonism including how Mormonism began, what Mormons believe, how they practice their faith, and what holidays they celebrate.
    ISBN 0-7377-3083-8 (alk. paper)
    1. Church of Jesus Christ of Latter-day Saints—Doctrines. 2. Mormons—Social life and customs. 3. Mormons—Religious life. I. Title. II. Series.
    BX8637.G46 2004
    289.3—dc22
                                                                    2004013636

Printed in the United States of America

CONTENTS

CHAPTER ONE

How Did Mormonism Begin?

Today, more than 11 million people worldwide are Mormons, but most prefer not to be called by that name. Their church, officially the Church of Jesus Christ of Latter-day Saints, or LDS, refers to its members as Saints. *Mormon,* however, is a commonly used term, and most church members accept it. The term refers to a great warrior-king in their holiest text, The Book of Mormon: Another Testament of Jesus Christ. Mormonism is the only Christian church that was founded in North America.

Days of Doubt and Suspicion

In the early 1800s, when the United States was barely fifty years old, much of the country was still frontier. Rugged individualists lived on the edges of civilization and eked out a living by their own hands. Among this mostly rural population, religion was important, and most people were devout Christians. However, many people were suspicious of organized churches. To solve their problems, many relied as much on folk medicine and folk magic (visions, omens, and magic spells) as they did on the Bible. One such family, the Smiths, lived in the Finger Lakes region of central New York State.

The Young Prophet

Joseph Smith Jr. (born December 23, 1805) was the fourth of nine children who migrated with their family

Joseph Smith Jr. is the founder of Mormonism, the only Christian church established in North America.

from Vermont in 1816, looking for fertile farmland. Joseph Jr., like many boys his age, had two burning religious questions in his mind—how to go to heaven, and which church was the right one. A highly intelligent and curious boy, he listened with interest to preachers of various churches. He was confused, however, because each thought their church was the only "right" one.

On an early spring morning in 1820, fourteen-year-old Joseph felt he needed guidance. Because he lived in a small house with a large family, finding a quiet place to pray was difficult, so he went into the woods near the family farm. There, in a quiet glen, he had what Mormons call the First Vision.

Joseph's First Vision

A pillar of light came down and rested upon him, he later recalled, and God's voice told him his sins had been forgiven. Then, from the pillar, God the Father and Jesus appeared. When he asked them which religious sect or denomination was right, they told him to join none. God told him his true church did not exist on the earth, that all churches since the death of his disciples had been corrupted and no longer spoke for him.

When Joseph awakened from his vision, he went home but told no one of his experience. He eventually confided in a few people, and he was criticized by clergy and by his neighbors for his claims.

A Visit from an Angel

Three years later, on September 21, 1823, Joseph, then seventeen, prayed once more for guidance, this time in

Moroni appears before Joseph Smith Jr. The angel visited Joesph many times.

his bedroom. According to his later recollection, his room became brighter than daylight and a figure clad in white robes appeared to him, hovering above the floor. This apparition identified himself as Moroni, an angel sent from God.

Moroni told Joseph his sins were still forgiven. He also said God had a mission for him, to prepare for the Second Coming of Christ, a mission that would bring him both glory and opposition. He told the young man that a book, written on golden plates, was hidden on a hill near the Smith farm.

Moroni said these plates contained the story of how one of the tribes of Israel, led by the prophet Lehi, had sailed to North America in 600 B.C. The plates also told how Jesus had later come to the New World after his resurrection, bringing this gospel to its inhabitants. The plates, six inches wide and eight inches long, were bound together into a book and inscribed with hiero-glyphic characters said to be "reformed Egyptian." Finally, he said there were special "seer" stones—called the Urim and Thummim—buried with the plates that would help Joseph translate them into modern English.

This is a replica of the golden plates with their mysterious script that Smith translated using special "seer" stones.

These stones were later described as two smooth, three-cornered diamonds set in glass and in a silver frame, much like a pair of eyeglasses.

The angel appeared three times during the night and once the following morning. During one visit, he said Joseph would be tempted by Satan to take the plates immediately but that he was to wait until God felt he was ready. In his final visit, Moroni commanded Joseph to tell his father about his visions and about the plates.

Going to the fields, Joseph told his father everything. His father, because of his belief in such mystical events, accepted his son's story and advised him to follow the angel's instructions.

Seeking the Plates

Despite Moroni's warning that he should not try to remove the objects from their hiding place until the time was right, Joseph visited the location he had seen in the visions later that morning, September 22, 1823. The low hill, Hill Cumorah, lay just east of the road between Palmyra and Canandaigua, three miles south and east of his home, near the town of Manchester, New York.

There, in scattered trees near the top of the western slope, Joseph dug through the earth and found a large stone. Prying it up, he found a stone box underneath containing the ancient relics. When he touched the contents of the box, he felt a strong physical shock, and the angel again appeared to him. Moroni scolded Joseph for giving in to temptation and told him he would not be able to take the stones until he had proved himself worthy.

Mormons celebrate on Hill Cumorah in New York, where the angel Moroni told Smith the plates and seer stones were hidden.

Joseph regularly visited the site. On each occasion, Moroni appeared, giving him further instruction. On September 22, 1827, four years after his first visit, Joseph and his new bride Emma visited the site. This time, Moroni allowed Joseph to take the plates. He wrapped the objects in cloth and took them home. Concerned that someone might try to steal the golden plates, Joseph and his bride soon traveled to her parents' house in Harmony, Pennsylvania. There, in a small bedroom, he translated what was written.

The Book of Mormon

To translate the plates, Joseph apparently did not have to look directly at them. Instead, he put the seer stones into a hat, buried his face into the hat, and dictated aloud what the stones revealed to him. He did not want anyone to observe this process, so he hung a blanket across the room. Joseph worked on one side with the plates and the stones. A scribe on the other side of the blanket wrote what Joseph dictated. After the translation was complete, the plates and stones disappeared. Joseph said the angel came and took them back.

With financial help, Joseph Smith then published the six-hundred-page translation of the plates, which he called The Book of Mormon, in March 1830. His father and brothers took the first five thousand copies and traveled from farm to farm in New York and northern Pennsylvania selling them. Eleven witnesses later attested to the existence of the plates, which they said had been

Smith reads from the Book of Mormon, his six-hundred-page translation of the plates published in 1830.

shown to them either by the angel Moroni or by Joseph. Their testimony is included at the beginning of every edition of the book.

This book, as Moroni had promised, is the historical record of how one of the tribes of Israel traveled to the Western Hemisphere around 600 B.C. It tells the sad tale of the descendants of the prophet Lehi, called Lamanites and Nephites, and how they fought with each other for centuries. It tells how Jesus Christ, after his resurrection, visited ancient America, preaching his message of love and brotherhood. This brought the two warring factions together and began two centuries of peace and harmony.

The story ends tragically, however, with a return to war and killing. In its final scenes, a great battle brings the total destruction of the Nephites and almost the same fate for the Lamanites. Moroni, the last Nephite prophet, recorded all that had happened and then, according to the book, hid the record for future generations. The spirit of this same prophet returned to earth in the 1820s to reveal the record to Joseph Smith Jr.

Because of its fascinating narrative—the story of an ancient American civilization whose existence was previously unknown—and because its religious teachings emphasized humankind's free will and America's destiny as a chosen land, interest in the book's message spread rapidly. Some accepted it as truth, but many believed it was fiction.

Founding the Church

In April, one month after the publication of The Book of Mormon, Joseph Smith and six followers organized the Church of Christ, later known by its present name,

Smith and his followers leave Independence, Missouri. The Mormons were forced to move frequently to escape persecution.

The Church of Jesus Christ of Latter-day Saints (LDS). Within months, its membership had grown into the thousands.

Escaping Persecution

Those who did not accept The Book of Mormon as a true gospel, however, believed it was a work of heresy and that it was somehow evil. Non-Mormons also feared the political and economic power of the rapidly growing group. As a result, Joseph and his church were criticized and persecuted. From its origins in New York, the LDS moved to Kirtland (now Kirtland Hills), Ohio, and to Independence, Missouri, in 1831. Persecution followed, along with violence on both sides, and in 1839, Joseph's flock again resettled, this time along the banks of the Mississippi River at Commerce, Illinois. They renamed the place Nauvoo, a Hebrew word meaning "beautiful place."

Defending themselves against local critics with a newly formed militia, the Mormons built Nauvoo into a city of more than twelve thousand by 1845. The church's problems did not go away, however. By the early 1840s, evidence that Joseph Smith had assumed kinglike power over his followers and rumors that Mormons had begun practicing polygamy (men having more than one wife) brought new criticism.

Polygamy had begun for the LDS around 1841, when Joseph claimed to have had another revelation from God. He later told church members that God had commanded Mormons to begin this Old Testament practice but to keep it secret. Between 1841 and 1844, Smith married many times. Some historians believe he married as many as forty-eight women.

News leaked to the general public, causing outrage. When one newspaper, the *Nauvoo Expositor,* published editorials condemning the practice, Smith ordered it destroyed. He and his brother, Hyrum, were then arrested for inciting a riot and jailed in Carthage, Illinois. On June 27, 1844, Smith and his brother were shot and killed by an anti-Mormon mob.

The Move to Utah

With the death of its prophet, the LDS began to falter. Splinter groups broke away. Most were small and did

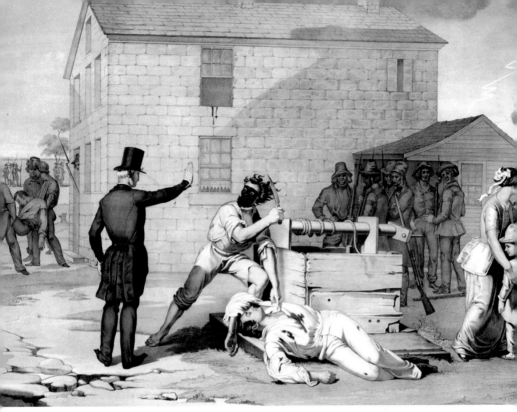

Joseph Smith lies shot to death as his brother's lifeless body is carried from the jail in Carthage, Illinois.

not last very long. The largest group remained near Independence, Missouri, and eventually became the Reorganized Church of Jesus Christ of Latter Day Saints.

The majority of Mormons followed Brigham Young (1801–1877), the second-highest official in the church, westward to Utah. Young, a native of Vermont, had converted to Mormonism in 1832. Because of his devotion to the LDS and his years of service, he was named head of the Council of Twelve Apostles, the governing body of the church, in 1841.

From 1846 to 1869, in the largest mass migration in American history, more than seventy thousand Mormons traveled fourteen hundred miles along what

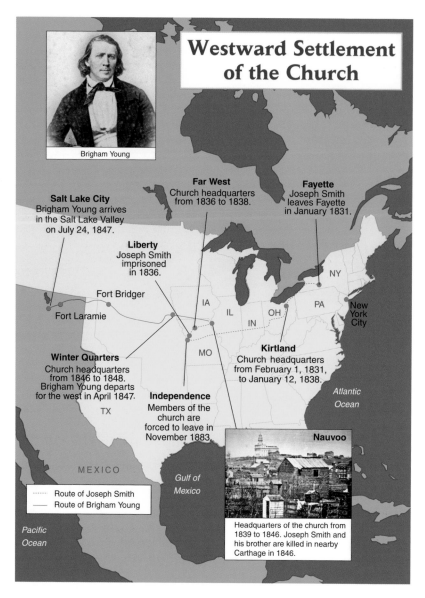

Westward Settlement of the Church

Brigham Young

Salt Lake City
Brigham Young arrives in the Salt Lake Valley on July 24, 1847.

Far West
Church headquarters from 1836 to 1838.

Fayette
Joseph Smith leaves Fayette in January 1831.

Liberty
Joseph Smith imprisoned in 1836.

NY

Fort Bridger

IA

Fort Laramie

IL

OH

IN

PA

New York City

Winter Quarters
Church headquarters from 1846 to 1848. Brigham Young departs for the west in April 1847.

MO

Kirtland
Church headquarters from February 1, 1831, to January 12, 1838.

Independence
Members of the church are forced to leave in November 1883.

TX

Atlantic Ocean

Nauvoo

MEXICO

Gulf of Mexico

------ Route of Joseph Smith
——— Route of Brigham Young

Pacific Ocean

Headquarters of the church from 1839 to 1846. Joseph Smith and his brother are killed in nearby Carthage in 1846.

came to be known as the Mormon Trail. Settling in the valley of the Great Salt Lake, they built Salt Lake City and found a place where they could live in relative peace and harmony.

In 1849 the Mormons established the state of Deseret, "land of the honey bee," including all of the present states of Utah and Nevada and parts of seven neighboring states. In 1850 the U.S. Congress established the region as the Territory of Utah and named Brigham Young its governor.

Polygamy continued to be criticized, even when the church was popular in Utah. The practice, made public in 1852 by Brigham Young, who had twenty wives, was condemned by the general public. In 1862 President Abraham Lincoln signed an antipolygamy law, but Mormons ignored it. After several more years of court cases and laws, the LDS finally gave in to pressure and voted to obey the law of the land, banning the practice in 1890. The LDS continued to condone polygamy, however, until 1907, when the church voted that anyone who openly practiced it would be excommunicated (removed from the church). Some Mormons, however, continued to ignore the ruling.

Despite this legal setback, Mormons have always stood by their religious beliefs, insisting on their right to worship their religion as they wish. Joseph Smith and his early followers endured criticism and persecution for their unusual beliefs, and that has not changed.

CHAPTER TWO

What Do I Believe?

Although Mormons share many beliefs with other Christian faiths, much of what they believe comes from the teachings of Prophet Joseph Smith. As their prophet, everything he taught is considered a revelation from God.

Sacred Texts

The primary sacred text of the church is The Book of Mormon, but in the years between its publication and Smith's death, he wrote other works he said also came directly from God. The Doctrine and Covenants, originally called The Book of Commandments, includes 135 revelations and other writings. The Pearl of Great Price, published in 1842, is the third book of LDS scripture. It includes the "Book of Abraham," supposedly written by the prophet Abraham and translated by Joseph Smith.

Toward the end of this text is a list of thirteen basic beliefs of Mormonism, the "Articles of Faith."

The fourth revered text for Mormons is the Holy Bible. However, Smith taught that some of the lessons included in the Bible had been mistranslated from their original language. As a result, he reinterpreted the King James Bible. He rewrote some passages to more closely conform to his writings and taught his followers to consider the Bible the word of God, but only as he had interpreted it.

Other differences in belief make the LDS unique among Christian faiths. Their key belief is that the Mormon Church is the only true Christian religion. They

Two brothers read from The Book of Mormon, one of the four sacred texts in the LDS.

believe they have restored the Christian church as Jesus and the apostles would have practiced it.

The Nature of God and Man

Mormons believe God the Father was once flesh and blood and that he became God through his own actions. They believe there have been an infinite number of gods through the ages, both male and female. They also believe that Jesus Christ was the first of many spirit children born of the Father and Mother and that he is the God referred to in the Old Testament as Jehovah. They teach that, because we are God's spirit children, each soul

A Mormon girl gazes at a poster of Jesus, the first of God's spiritual children according to Mormon belief.

can attain Godlike status in the afterlife.

Most Christian churches preach that each soul is created by God at birth but that it lives eternally after physical death. Mormons believe each soul lived with God as spirit before birth and that, after death, the soul returns to God. To Mormons, life on earth is a dress rehearsal to prepare souls for the next world. According to LDS doctrine, God made several commandments concerning what people should do with their lives on earth—grow in knowledge, develop talents and gifts, follow His callings, exercise free will (make their own decisions), and establish stable family relationships.

Degrees of Glory

Mormons have a complex understanding of the afterlife. Mormons believe people are judged according to how well they have obeyed God's laws and are placed into one of three "degrees of glory." The telestial kingdom, the lowest level, is reserved for those who rejected the gospel of Jesus Christ and committed serious sins for which they did not ask forgiveness. Those who live in this kingdom must first pass through a period of torment and suffering. People in the telestial kingdom are forever separated from God the Father and from Jesus Christ.

The second level is the terrestial kingdom, for Mormons who have lived honorable lives but who have not followed gospel teachings completely. They are in the presence of Jesus, but still separated from God the Father.

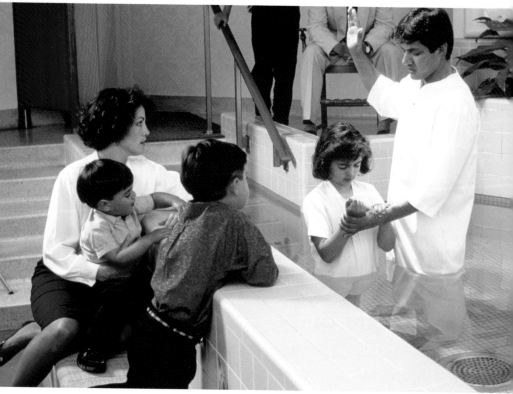

A girl is baptized as her family watches. Mormons believe that nobody may enter heaven without being baptized.

The highest degree of glory, the one Mormons strive for, is the celestial kingdom. It is only for Mormons who have fully repented of sin, been baptized according to Mormon ritual, and married in a Mormon temple. Small children who die before their eighth birthday, the age of accountability, also go to the celestial kingdom.

Other Teachings

Another unique belief of the LDS is baptism of the dead. Since Mormons consider theirs the only true church and the only pathway to heaven, ancestors who died before Joseph Smith's revelations and teachings could not be in heaven. Instead, they must be in a sort of purgatory, waiting for final salvation. Mormons believe the living can stand in and be baptized for people who have already died. These spirits, still fully alert, are free to accept or reject the Mormon gospel.

Finally, Smith taught that the body is sacred and should be cared for accordingly. A person's body clothes the immortal soul. In 1833, in a passage known as "The Word of Wisdom," Smith wrote that the physical body is a precious gift, and to keep it healthy, a person should eat a balanced diet, get plenty of exercise, and avoid tobacco, alcohol, drinks containing caffeine (coffee, tea, and most soft drinks), and illegal drugs.

Young Mormons visit a statue of Christ in a temple room designed to look like the celestial kingdom.

Today, the concept of free will, being able to make decisions that will affect getting into heaven, seems obvious. In Joseph Smith's time, however, many churches preached that man's fate was preordained—already decided by God—and that there was little people could do to change it. Smith's teachings about free will became quite popular. The concept that Godlike status is available to all humans and that it depends on how well a person follows the teachings of The Book of Mormon, the Bible, and the other teachings of Joseph Smith makes the way Mormons practice their faith all the more important to salvation.

CHAPTER THREE

How Do I Practice My Faith?

The LDS has no professional clergy. Instead, religious services are led by laypersons—persons not formally trained in religion. Every worthy male above the age of twelve can be ordained as a member of the Aaronic priesthood. At the age of eighteen, he advances into the Melchizedek priesthood. Members of these priesthoods play various roles in Mormon worship services. Because any male may become a Mormon priest, it follows that Mormons believe any male can also become a prophet. A prophet is a seer with the ability to predict the future and a receiver of revelations from God.

Church Organization

Despite the lack of professional clergy and the church's doctrine of free will, the church is governed in a highly centralized and authoritarian way by the general

Gordon B. Hinkley became the fifteenth president of the LDS in 1995. Mormons consider their president to be a prophet.

authorities of the church, commonly known as "the brethren." At the top of this hierarchy is the president, considered to be a prophet. He chooses a first and second counselor. Together, they make up the First Presidency.

Next is the Council of the Twelve Apostles. These men hold their positions for life and are ranked according to seniority. When the president dies, the leader of the council takes over his position. Each of these officials, though secure in his position, is unanimously "sustained," or reelected, by the church membership at annual conferences in Salt Lake City.

Below the Council of the Twelve Apostles is the First Quorum of the Seventy. Members of this administrative body serve to the age of seventy. In the 1990s, due to the growth of the LDS, church leaders created the Second, Third, Fourth, and Fifth Quorums of the Seventy, responsible for such things as the church's missionary programs, relief agencies, and Sunday school programs in various parts of the world. Members of these quorums typically serve terms of five and one-half years and oversee LDS divisions called stakes. These each contain two thousand to ten thousand members. Stakes are further subdivided into wards, each with five hundred to six hundred members, supervised by lesser officials.

Central church authority rests with the First Presidency and the Council of the Twelve Apostles, and each year the church publishes the *General Handbook of Instructions,* outlining its policy. Copies of this handbook are numbered and given only to those in authority in the church. Few regular members ever see it.

Religious Services

Religious services in Mormonism are performed in temples, tabernacles, chapels, and homes. Most striking to visitors not familiar with Mormonism is the absence of the traditional Christian cross. This is due to Mormons' focus on Christ's life and teachings. They believe the cross focuses too much on his death.

Houses of Worship

Most sacred for Mormons is the temple. A typical Mormon temple resembles a luxury hotel, with any number of rooms for special ceremonies, such as "sealings" (marriages for eternity), ordinations, and baptisms, both for the living and for the dead. Each temple, though, has only one celestial room, where the faithful go to meditate and pray.

The approximately fifty Mormon temples around the world are not open to the public and are not meeting places or churches in the ordinary sense. In the temple, the highest doctrines of the church are taught to those deemed worthy, but not all qualify to enter. Only 10 to 30 percent of Mormons have been granted a "temple recommend," a card renewed each year allowing them to enter the temple.

Those who have received their temple recommend and completed a ceremony called an "endowment" promise to give 10 percent of their income as a tithe, to serve in whatever capacity is asked of them, and to be loyal to the church. During the endowment ceremony, each member receives the "garment"—sacred underwear they are to wear day and night. This can be one- or two-piece cotton underwear, with religious symbols. Mormons wear the garment as an unseen reminder of who they are. Some even feel the garment protects them from harm.

Mormon tabernacles are not as secret or as sacred as temples. In tabernacles, everyone is welcome to attend public religious services and musical programs. The best-known Mormon tabernacle, located in Salt Lake City, was completed in 1867 and seats over ten thousand people. It is home to one of the largest pipe organs in the world. The tabernacle is also the home of the world-famous Mormon Tabernacle Choir, which has toured the world since 1893 and served as a goodwill ambassador between Mormons and people of other faiths.

The Mormon Tabernacle Choir performs in the Salt Lake City tabernacle. The choir has toured the world since 1893.

Most weekly Mormon religious ceremonies are performed in local chapels. These services are similar to other Protestant church services in some ways, but different in others. Mormons dress in their best clothes and gather on Sunday mornings to sing hymns, pray, and listen to religious messages. Since Mormon churches do not have trained preachers, each service may be different. Instead of the traditional sermon, most services feature individual testimonies, sometimes from church members less than ten years old. Services may also include the blessing and naming of babies or the blessing of the sick by members of the lay priesthood. The only ceremony common to all Mormon worship services is Holy Communion, performed each week using bread and water to invoke the memory of Christ's blood and body.

Walking the Walk

Outside the churches, Mormons practice their religion in almost everything they do. Mondays are reserved for "family nights." Families spend time together reading from the Bible or The Book of Mormon, playing games, doing skits or crafts, or talking about the week's events. This time is important for Mormon families, central to their belief in the importance of stable family relationships. This family focus has been carried to the general public through countless television, radio, and print advertisements, encouraging family values.

Their family relationships, along with their belief in baptism of the dead, have led Mormons to create the

Members of a Mormon family work together in their vegetable garden.
Family activities are very important to Mormons.

most extensive genealogical library in the world. In Little
Cottonwood Canyon, twelve miles from downtown Salt
Lake City, under hundreds of feet of solid granite, lie
huge rooms containing the genealogical record of most
of the earth's population. People of every faith come
here to research their ancestry.

Mormons are also a practical people, always pre-
pared for emergencies. Each family is instructed to keep
a year's supply of food in case of emergencies. The
Mormon Relief Agency, founded in 1842, is designed
to relieve the suffering of anyone who requests help.
Women in the LDS participate in this organization, car-
ing for the sick, visiting homes, instructing women
about food preservation, hygiene, and cooking and can-
ning food for relief missions.

Youth activities include the Young Men's and the Young Women's Mutual Improvement Associations, called the M.I.A. These provide supervised training in drama, speech, music, dance, the arts, crafts, and athletics. The Young Men's Association also conducts an extensive Boy Scout program. Brigham Young University, in Provo, Utah, with more than thirty-two thousand students, is the largest church-operated university in the United States. The majority of its students are LDS members.

Mormons are also active in missionary work, with over twenty-five thousand full-time missionaries scattered throughout the world. All young Mormons—men at the age of nineteen and women at twenty-one—are required to serve as missionaries, either in the United States or overseas, for one and one-half to two years. Along with older Mormon missionaries, these young people must communicate their beliefs to others. Whether in the temple, in the tabernacle, in the chapel, in the home, or on the street, Mormons take their faith seriously.

CHAPTER FOUR

What Holidays Do I Celebrate?

Members of the LDS, like Christians the world over, celebrate the two main holidays associated with Jesus Christ—Christmas and Easter. The LDS regards these events as the most spiritually significant days in history because they commemorate the birth, death, and resurrection of Christ.

Christmas and Easter

Mormons celebrate Christmas and Easter on the same dates as other Christian churches—Christmas on December 25 and Easter on the Sunday following the first full moon after the spring equinox. Mormons celebrate these holidays in much the same way as other Christians, with one exception. Mormons do not fast during Lent, the period between Ash Wednesday and Easter, as some Christians do.

During Christmas a Mormon family dressed in biblical clothing reenacts the birth of Jesus in their home.

Mormons commemorate Easter Sunday with special church services, often at sunrise. During the service, lay leaders read scripture from the Bible or from The Book of Mormon. Local LDS wards put on Easter pageants, depicting the suffering, death, and resurrection of Christ, or stage Easter cantatas, musical programs with an Easter theme. For these celebrations, chapels are often decorated with white lilies, symbolizing life.

Pioneer Day

One holiday unique to the LDS is Pioneer Day on July 24. This holiday commemorates the arrival of the first Mormon settlers to the Salt Lake Valley in 1847. Church members worldwide honor their pioneer heritage on that day. Most large-scale celebrations, however, are held in the western United States, with huge parades and festivals, devotionals, sporting events, feasts, dances, concerts, rodeos, art shows, and reunions.

General Conference

Although not technically a Mormon holiday, one event held twice a year is significant to LDS members. On the first weekend in April and the first weekend in October, the church holds its General Conference for all members. Thousands travel to Salt Lake City to witness this event. Even the Salt Lake City tabernacle is not large enough to hold all who want to attend. Others

Modern-day Mormons pull handcarts along a road in Vermont on Pioneer Day to commemorate the Mormons' westward trek.

Mormon Celebrations Throughout the Year

General Conference
Biannual event in Salt Lake City connecting the global community of church members.

Easter Sunday
Celebrates the resurrection of Jesus.

JANUARY   FEBRUARY   MARCH   APRIL   MAY   JUNE

watch and listen by closed-circuit television in other buildings or on blankets spread in Temple Square.

Inside the tabernacle, the current president, members of the Council of the Twelve Apostles, and other general authorities give talks about such topics as the importance of tithing, commitment to the family, and loyalty to the church. Over thirty-five hundred LDS stake centers around the world receive the meeting live, via satellite. More than twelve hundred cable television and radio stations broadcast conference sessions. Videotapes and audiotapes of the talks are distributed throughout the world.

Hill Cumorah Pageant

Another important event has taken place each summer since 1937—the Hill Cumorah Pageant in Palmyra, New

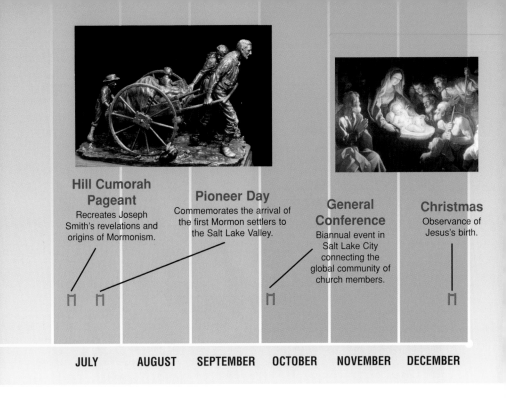

Hill Cumorah Pageant
Recreates Joseph Smith's revelations and origins of Mormonism.

Pioneer Day
Commemorates the arrival of the first Mormon settlers to the Salt Lake Valley.

General Conference
Biannual event in Salt Lake City connecting the global community of church members.

Christmas
Observance of Jesus's birth.

JULY   AUGUST   SEPTEMBER   OCTOBER   NOVEMBER   DECEMBER

York. Every year, a cast of over six hundred recreates the story of Joseph Smith's revelations, his discovery of the golden plates, his translation of The Book of Mormon, and the founding of the LDS church. The pageant takes place on the slopes of Hill Cumorah, where Smith unearthed the golden plates.

Each year, usually in mid-July, over one hundred thousand people watch this dramatic presentation on the origins of Mormonism, called "America's Witness for Christ." The annual production is one of the most elaborate religious pageants in the world.

Today, Mormonism is the fastest growing Christian denomination in the world. It took 117 years—from 1830 to 1947—for the church to reach 1 million members. It took only thirteen additional years to double that number. Presently, the LDS claims 5,310,598

A group of Mormons marches in a 2001 New York City parade.
Mormonism is the world's fastest-growing Christian denomination.

members who attend services in almost every nation of the world.

The Mormon Church has changed since its founding. Doctrines have adapted to modern society and to obey the law of the land. The focus of LDS doctrine is the family. Many believe this is responsible for Mormonism's rapid growth. Whatever the reasons, the Church of Jesus Christ of Latter-day Saints is, as Joseph Smith envisioned it, fulfilling the mission entrusted to him almost two hundred years ago.

FOR FURTHER EXPLORATION

Books

Claudia Bushman and Richard Bushman, *Building the Kingdom: A History of Mormons in America*. New York: Oxford University Press, 2001. These two historians at Columbia University have written a balanced, informative, and concise study of Mormonism, focusing on everyday experiences of ordinary Mormons. They also discuss ways the LDS has changed during its history.

Veronica Doubleday, *Salt Lake City*. Austin, TX: Silver Burdett, 1994. The story of the LDS and the founding of Salt Lake City. Chapters on Joseph Smith and Brigham Young, as well as the church's traditions, ceremonies, genealogy, and welfare program.

Cory Gideon Gunderson, *Brigham Young: Pioneer and Prophet*. Mankato, MN: Capstone, 2002. The life of Brigham Young, from his childhood in Vermont to his leadership of the Mormon Church, including the migration to Utah in 1846. Informative, well illustrated, and well organized. Includes time line, glossary, and bibliography.

Maxine Hanks, *Mormon Faith in America.* New York: Facts On File, 2003. The basic beliefs and church history of the LDS and its expansion throughout the world. Also short biographical sketches of famous Mormon Americans. Black-and-white photographs.

Carol Rust Nash, *The Mormon Trail and the Latter-day Saints in American History.* Berkeley Heights, NJ: Enslow, 1999. Explores the founding of the LDS, its persecution and migration, the church's legacy, and its present role in society.

Lynda Cory Robinson, *Boys Who Became Prophets.* Salt Lake City, UT: Deseret, 2000. This Mormon publication tells the life stories of fifteen LDS prophets, from Joseph Smith Jr. to the current president, Gordon B. Hinckley.

Charnan Simon, *Brigham Young: Mormon and Pioneer.* New York: Scholastic Library, 1998. An objective biography. Relatively easy to read, with short chapters followed by time lines.

Jean Kinney Williams, *The Mormons.* Danbury, CT: Franklin Watts, 1996. An in-depth narrative, covering the background, development, culture, and current status of the LDS. Large, captioned black-and-white photographs.

Gayla Wise, *I Am a Latter-day Saint.* New York: Rosen, 2003. An introduction to the beliefs and practices of Mormonism through the eyes of a young Saint.

Web Sites

All About Mormons (www.mormons.org). The most comprehensive and accurate site on the Internet about the Mormon religion.

The Church of Jesus Christ of Latter-day Saints: Official Homepage (www.lds.org). Basic information about the church, including membership numbers and information about the missionary program and temples, along with the religion's basic beliefs.

Mormon.Com: An Internet Resource for Latter-day Saints (www.mormon.com). An attractive and informative site aimed at members of the LDS, but also a good source to learn about Mormons and church activities.

INDEX

PICTURE CREDITS

ABOUT THE AUTHOR

Charles George taught history and Spanish in Texas public schools for sixteen years. He now lives with his wife of thirty-three years, Linda, in the mountains of New Mexico. Together, they have written nearly fifty young adult and children's nonfiction books. Charles has written two Lucent books, *Life Under the Jim Crow Laws* and *Civil Rights*. For KidHaven Press, he has written *The Holocaust*, part of the History of the World series, and *Buddhist* and *Hindu* for the What Makes Me A?* series. He and Linda also wrote *Texas* for the Seeds of a Nation series.